Gardening WITH THE EXPERTS

VEGETABLE GARDENS

Gardening
WITH THE EXPERTS

VEGETABLE GARDENS

MARY MOODY

HARLAXTON
PUBLISHING

Published by Harlaxton Publishing Ltd
2 Avenue Road, Grantham, Lincolnshire, NG31 6TA, United Kingdom.
A Member of the Weldon International Group of Companies.

First published in 1992.
Reprinted 1993

Publishing Manager: Robin Burgess
Project Coordinator: Mary Moody
Editor: Christine Mackinnon
Illustrator: Kathie Baxter Smith
Designed & produced for the publisher by Phillip Mathews Publishers
Produced in Singapore by Imago

British Library Cataloguing-in-Publication data.
A catalogue record for this book is available from the British Library.
Title: Gardening with the Experts: Vegetable Gardens
ISBN:1 85837 035 3

CONTENTS

INTRODUCTION

Growing vegetables is one of the most rewarding aspects of gardening that is not difficult nor as time consuming as many people imagine.

Even in a small space it is possible to grow a wide range of nutritious vegetables; an average back garden has the scope to produce a substantial crops that will last for most of the year.

There are valid reasons for adding a vegetable garden, fruit trees or herb patch to the general garden landscape. Increased knowledge about the effects of pesticides and chemical fertilisers on the food chain is a concern to many families. It is possible to supplement the average family pantry with home-grown vegetables that are free from chemicals and rich in nutrient value due to their freshness.

A reasonable quantity of vegetables can be produced even in a small to average size back garden. Most species can be grown much more closely together than generally indicated if the soil is rich, constantly replenished with organic matter and a good watering regime is maintained.

In larger gardens, semi-self sufficiency can be achieved across a wide range of

A well-organised gardener can produce a good yield with minimal effort.

Opposite: Plant crops that are high in nutrition, yet popular with the whole family.

7

Always locate the vegetable patch in the most open, sunny place in the garden.

vegetables if the garden is efficiently planned and maintained.

Fruit production requires more space, it is therefore more difficult to maintain a constant supply. With bottling and freezing of certain crops a steady supply can be maintained through the winter months.

No matter how small, every garden should accommodate a small area to grow a few vegetables.

Position
The most important prerequisite for growing vegetables is an abundance of sunlight. A vegetable garden needs to be located in the most open and sunny part of the garden, away from overhanging trees or shade from buildings.

This often means that the vegetable garden has to be centrally sited — a prospect that does not appeal to some gardeners. However, if the vegetable or herb patch is well cared for there is no reason why it can not be just as attractive as any ornamental garden.

Think in terms of a kitchen garden that is located within easy access of the kitchen door. A small pathway, lined on either side with herbs, can lead to a bed containing well-mulched rows of vegetables in season.

Vine crops, or root crops like potatoes, can be grown in more isolated corners, near the compost for example, while crops that need more general maintenance can be positioned in the main bed.

When choosing a site for the vegetable garden avoid large, well-established trees. Not only will they cast unwanted shadows, but they will also compete for moisture and nutrients from the soil.

Consider the need or some crops for shelter against prevailing winds. This can be provided by a slow-growing hedge of small bushes, for example.

Healthy crops are the result of soil building and careful maintenance.

GARDEN PLANNING

To get the most from the available space in the vegetable garden, first draw up a garden plan. Factors to be considered when making a plan include companion planting; succession planting and crop rotation. The general rule is to alternate root crops and leaf crops, ensuring that the lower growing species are kept at the front of the garden where sunlight will not be blocked by larger plants.

Group perennials such as rhubarb, asparagus and strawberries together in one bed where they can be mulched easily in winter time.

Allow sufficient space between rows to walk, weed and harvest. Remember,

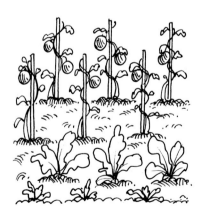

Root and vine crops grown together.

however, that if the soil is rich with organic matter and well watered, plants can be grown quite close together. Keep in mind that tall-growing crops like sweet corn, climbing beans and tomatoes should be positioned towards the back of the garden.

Use graph paper to draw a ground plan for the garden starting with the spring growth. Record how long each group of plants takes to mature in your particular climate. After several seasons a pattern will emerge.

Companion planting
Companion planting is a farming and gardening practice that is centuries old, but still can be applied with great success to a modern vegetable garden.

The basic principles of companion planting are really very simple. Certain plants grow harmoniously together because their specific needs complement each other. The complex relationship between these plants can be explained scientifically, but in nature it happens spontaneously.

Companion planting works because:
1. Shallow-rooted plants thrive when planted near deep-rooted species. The deeper rooted plants break down and loosen the soil and provide better drainage for those with shallow roots.
2. Leaf crops do better when planted next

Avoid planting the same crops in the same position year after year.

to root crops because they are not competing for the same ground space or specific nutrients (leaf crops need nitrogen!).

3. Tall-growing species can provide shade and shelter for smaller plants.

4. Species with different water and nutrient requirements are good together as they do not directly compete with each other.

5. Certain species have roots which give off nitrogen and make it available for nearby plants that require quantities of nitrogen.

6. Certain species exude aromas that repel insects, or are good when planted next to plants that are susceptible to attack.

By practising the basic rules of companion planting when planning the layout of a vegetable garden, you will help to create a healthy environment which in turn will produce plants that are less vulnerable to disease and insect pests.

Interplanting

Make the most of gaps in the garden to grow a few extra plants. The space between large crops, such as tomatoes, can be filled with small rows of root crops such as carrots or beetroot. Marrows and other rambling vine crops can be planted on the edge of a clump of corn, and allowed to wind their way through the clump (works as a companion plant because the corn shades the marrows whose leaves stop the soil from drying out around the corn).

Interplanting only works successfully if the soil is rich and the garden is main-

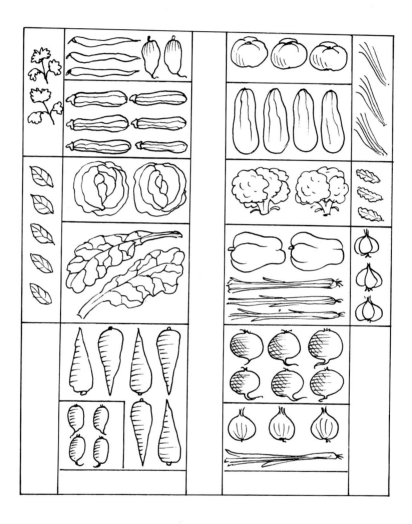

A simple ground plan for growing a variety of root and leaf crops to feed an average family.

PARSLEY	BROCCOLI followed by CORN, planted with LETTUCE & RADISHES		PARSLEY
DILL	PEAS followed by BEANS	TOMATOES planted with COS LETTUCE, RADISHES, or SHALLOTS	CHIVES
SAVORY	SPINACH followed by BEANS followed by CAULIFLOWER, BROCCOLI	CABBAGE followed by SQUASH	DILL
OREGANO	early LETTUCE followed by MELONS	MUSTARD GREENS followed by CAPSICUM planted with LETTUCE	BASIL
MARIGOLDS	PEAS followed by CUCUMBERS planted with RADISHES	BEETS followed by BROAD BEANS	MARIGOLDS
MARIGOLDS	CARROTS (succession planting)	BROCCOLI followed by BEANS followed by TURNIPS	MARIGOLDS
	MARJORAM	TARRAGON	

A workable example of simple crop rotation and interplanting of leaf, vine and root crops.

Above: Railway sleepers make an excellent timber garden edging for the vegetable patch.
Below: Built up beds improve drainage. Here vegetables and annuals are in close proximity.

tained to prevent weed growth.

In poorer soils, or areas with low rainfall, Interplanting will cause too much competition for moisture and nutrients and none of the plants will grow successfully.

Succession planting

Succession planting is the common-sense way of getting the best from the garden.

It involves planting crops in stages rather than all at once. Instead of planting a large quantity of each vegetable at one time, small amounts are planted every fortnight to ensure a steady supply of fresh crops.

This is especially important with leaf crops during summer, which will all bolt and go to seed if planted at the same time. Instead of planting thirty lettuce in one day, plant ten lettuce every fortnight and they will mature and be ready for harvesting over a much longer period. Without succession planting all thirty lettuce will need harvesting at the same time, creating a glut.

Succession planting saves ground space because as each row is harvested a new crop can replace it.

In a cool to cold climate, succession planting will be limited by the length of the spring and summer growing season.

Crops like tomatoes or capsicum need to be planted in early spring if they are to have time to mature before autumn.

In warmer climates, with a less dramatic difference between seasons, succession planting can be practised all year round, providing a steady supply of fresh crops.

Crop rotation

This is yet another gardening practice that has been used for centuries. Long before scientific explanations were available it was understood that planting crops in the same field year after year gave poor results.

Soil-borne diseases could be transferred from one season's crop to the next, so a rest or fallow period became necessary.

Although not used as often as it should be in agriculture, crop rotation is certainly advisable in the vegetable garden. Certain crops demand specific nutrients from the soil, and if these crops are grown in the same spot season after season the soil balance will be depleted.

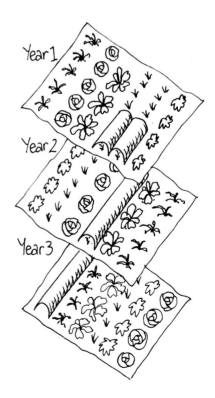

A *simple three-year crop rotation plan.*

Allow space in the garden for the planting of successive crops.

*Raising seedlings at home
is the most economical method of
vegetable gardening.*

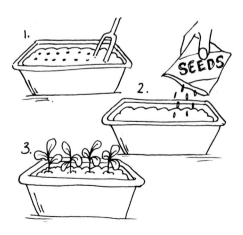

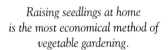

Leaf crops draw nitrogen from the soil in large quantities. Therefore a leaf crop should always be followed by a root crop that does not demand as much nitrogen.

In your garden always plan to change the layout every year so that plants from one family group are not always positioned in the same place, for example cabbages, brussel sprouts and cauliflowers all belong to the same family group and should be moved every year. Using this system, nutrient deficiencies can be prevented as different plant groups take different nutrients from the soil. By rotating root and leaf crops a balance is achieved. Also, pH requirements vary from plant to plant.

Do not position acid-loving plants in ground that has been limed. Follow a heavy-feeding crop with one that requires less nutrient from the soil.

SOIL IMPROVEMENT

To create a productive garden the starting point is rich, friable soil. Vegetables are generally heavy feeders and therefore require good soil. Plants grown in poor soil are much more susceptible to insect attack and disease infestation, they tend to grow slowly and become woody and tough.

Types of Soil

To improve the soil, first establish the texture and drainage qualities.

Soils fall into the following categories:

Sandy: Soil which is light and easy to cultivate but has the disadvantage of losing moisture too quickly, becoming dry and often hard-caked on the surface.

It is difficult to form into a shape. It will crack and crumble. If you try to bend the shape it will fall apart.

Add plenty of well-rotted manures, compost or other soil building materials such as rotted leaves.

Loam: This is the ideal soil to find in your garden, as it is easy to cultivate yet holds moisture well.

Good loam has neither too much sand nor too much clay content. It will form a shape much more easily, and hold together quite well. However when you try and bend the shape it will crack slightly.

Clay: This type of soil is heavy and hard to work. Water takes a long time to drain away after rain or watering.

To test the texture of your soil take a small quantity — half a handful — lightly moisten it. The object of this test is to form the soil into a sausage shape, then lightly bend it, to determine its structure.

To improve the structure and texture of the soil the addition of plenty of organic matter is essential. There are clay breaking substances, such as gypsum, which are useful to help break down clay particles.

Drainage problems

Drainage can affect the health of some vegetables which will rot in poorly drained conditions. Areas of the garden with poor drainage need to be corrected.

Badly drained soil is easy to identify as the structure tends to be heavy and too frequently very wet.

If you are uncertain try this simple test. Dig a hole to a depth of about 60 cm (2 ft) and fill it with water until the entire area appears saturated.

If drainage is adequate the water in the hole should drain away within a few hours.

If water remains in the hole until the next day, poor drainage is the reason.

Poor drainage can be solved in various ways. The most simple is to improve the texture by adding plenty of organic matter such as manures and compost, or to create built-up garden beds that incorporate their own drainage.

Rich, well-drained soil is essential for leaf crops such as silver beet.

As good drainage is important for the growing of most vegetable crops, vegetable gardeners frequently use built-up beds.

An alternative solution for correcting drainage is to lay underground drainage pipes to take water away from plant roots.

This is really not as difficult as it seems, although digging trenches can be quite backbreaking. The idea is to lay pipes at a slight angle sloping downwards.

When too much water hits the subsoil it drains through a bed of gravel into the pipes, then is taken away to lower ground.

Organic gardeners sometimes plant deep-rooted species like comfrey or lupins in the badly drained region. When mature the plants can be chopped with a spade and dug into the ground together with lots of well-rotted manure. In the meantime, as the plants mature, the roots will have helped to break up the subsoil.

Organic compost and manures are the most effective soil builders.

A ground-level compost heap requires frequent watering and turning.

Work the soil when it is lightly damp — never when it is either dry or waterlogged.

Soil building: Generally speaking healthy soil is the result of several years of building with organic matter.

Regardless of the original soil condition, the addition of composts and manures will result in a marked improvement and generally make gardening much easier.

Apart from adding valuable nutrients to the soil, incorporating organic matter improves texture, structure, drainage and makes cultivation easier.

It is best to incorporate composts and manures into the garden soil prior to planting. An additional application after planting as a thick mulch layer will gradually break down into the soil, releasing nutrients and decomposing to improve texture and drainage as it does so.

A layered compost that includes manures will break down quickly, especially if the ingredients have been shredded.

General Maintenance

Vegetable gardens are considered time-consuming because most species of vegetables are annuals, therefore they must be labour intensive needing frequent planting, mulching, weeding, watering, feeding and harvesting.

A well-planned garden should take no more than a routine two hour maintenance per week for most of the year.

There are times, early spring, when work may be greater as time is needed to clear winter debris and plant summer crops.

On a regular basis, a few hours of work should keep the garden in good order!

Planting: To keep a steady supply of vegetables, routine planting of either seeds or seedlings is required.

Plant according to the seasons, only plant a consumable quantity of each variety at a time to prevent over supply (see Succession planting).

Weeding: Routinely keep weeds down between rows with a hoe or cultivator.

Water the ground well the day before to make weeding easier. Take care not to disturb the root systems of young plants.

Mulching: Excellent to prevent weed growth and to prevent the soil surface from

Keep planting throughout the season, to ensure a steady supply of vegetables.

Opposite: Mulch young established vegetables to keep weeds down. Here grass clippings have been used.

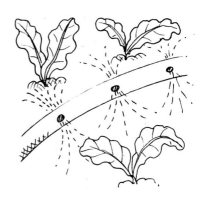

Sprinklers are good for covering large areas.

A soaker hose will water at ground level, which is preferable for some species (such as tomatoes).

drying out. Mulch between crop rows and around plants with a thick layer of well-rotted manure (poultry, cow or horse) then top with a layer of grass clippings. Maintain the mulch layer every few weeks.

Feeding: Healthy vegetables demand fast and steady growth. Even rich soil will not produce perfect results unless a routine feeding regime is followed.

Leaf crops should be fed with a liquid fertiliser every fortnight from the time they become established.

Root crops can be fed steadily by mulching with well-rotted manure, and a side dressing of blood and bone.

Tomatoes have specific requirements and should be fed with a balanced tomato fertilizer every few weeks.

Watering: Vegetable gardens need to be watered every day in summer, especially if a warm wind is blowing, but less frequently

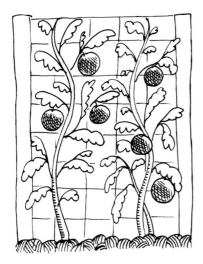

Provide support for climbing species.or those, such as tomatoes, which bear heavy fruits.

in spring and autumn. Do not sprinkle the surface but water deeply to encourage roots to travel downwards.

Tomatoes, capsicum and eggplants should be watered at ground level, while others can be watered with an overhead sprinkler.

Staking: Tall species, such as tomatoes, may require a wooden stake for support. Keep a check that the plant is loosely tied as it grows, make sure the ties are not so tight that stems are damaged.

Climbing beans and cucumbers need some support, such as a trellis or wire, to climb as they grow. Try to position these towards the back of the garden, where they will not throw a shadow on small-growing species.

Pests and disease: Check plants regularly to detect problems before they get out of hand. Look at the backs of leaves for signs of insect infestation, then either wipe or spray with warm soapy water.

Early intervention will make management of pests much easier. Many insect pests, such as aphids, can be removed manually or hosed off with water rather than using chemical sprays.

THE CROPS

LEAF CROPS

To be light and crisp leaf crops should be grown quickly, with plenty of watering and feeding to maintain fast and steady growth.

Celery (*Apium graveolens*): This crop requires plenty of water and regular feeding to provide the rapid growth necessary for success. Stalks should be blanched to remain light green, and this involves either wrapping the base of each plant in newspaper, or planting seedlings in a trench, then gradually filling around the base with soil as the plant grows.

Cress (*Lepidium sativum*): An excellent crisp green for salads, cress is best produced under glass for rapid tender shoots in a fine soil, or on an absorbent pad, which eliminated gritty soil particles. Feed fortnightly, and harvest by clipping back with sharp scissors. It only takes a few weeks to begin producing sufficient for a daily salad!

Dandelion (*Taraxacum officinale*): Although considered a weed, dandelions are very nutritious and can be used in salads most effectively. Collect seeds and sow a small patch in the vegetable garden — requires no special care or attention.

Endive (*Cichorium endivia*): A late autumn alternative to lettuce, should be blanched before use and protected from frost. A strong flavoured green which has become more popular in recent years, it is high in iron.

Lettuce (*Lactuca sativa*): Choose from many varieties of cos and cabbage lettuce. Lettuce can be grown most of the year, using greenhouses in cool regions, begin outdoor sowing in spring when frost danger has passed.

Endive is a leafy green with a crisp, sharp flavour.

Provide protection from predators such as birds.
Here strips of cloth attached to string provide a visual barrier.

Silver beet (*Beta vulgaris cicla*): Easy to grow, it is an excellent crop for small gardens because it produces a vitamin-rich yield in a small space. Leaves can be harvested individually by cutting with a sharp knife right at the base. In warm regions, plant seeds every month for a year round supply.

Spinach (*Spinacia oleracea*): Prefers a cool to cold climate and rich, moist soil. Plant as a catch-crop between rows of beans, cabbages or leeks. Outer leaves should be ready for picking after only eight weeks.

THE BRASSICAS

Most Brassicas are heavy feeders and need to be grown quickly to produce tender results as slow growth will result in woody crops. Brassicas are prone to insect attack by cabbage moth, caterpillars and other leaf-eating pests. If well grown they should be able to withstand the onslaught with a few preventative measures (derris dust is a good all-round deterrent).

Brussel sprouts (*Brassica oleracea* 'Gemmifera'): These take up a bit of space in the garden but are a good crop for autumn and winter months. Sprouts grow best in cool to cold areas, where seeds can

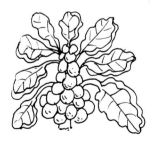

Brussel sprouts are heavy feeders.

Water and feed leaf crops regularly, and protect them from snails and slugs.

be sown from late spring to late summer, however, in warm to tropical districts sowing should be left until late summer.
Cabbage (*Brassica oleracea* 'Capitata'): There are many varieties to choose from, including some that crop after only seven or eight weeks.

The leaves have a high water content so regular watering and feeding is necessary. Cabbages can be grown all year round with successive planting, but does not stand severe frost.

There are varieties to suit all regions.
Cauliflower (*Brassica oleracea* 'Botrytis'): Cauliflowers are very heavy feeders, so add lots of manure to the soil before planting, and mulch well. Seeds can be sown in late

summer in most regions, and in warmer climates extra watering will be needed.

When the heads begin to form, tie the outer leaves together to cover them, as this will keep the heads snowy white. Broccoli is a close relative.
Kohl-rabi (*Brassica oleracea gongyloïdes*): Tasting a bit like a cross between a swede and a turnip, it forms a bulb above the ground, topped with cream and purple foliage. Small form is suited as a catch-crop, the larger is coarse and grown for cattle fodder.
Relatively easy to grow, both bulb and foliage are edible, and should be ready to pick in about eight weeks after sowing.
Swedes (*Brassica rutabaga*): Swedes are a

Opposite: Harvest cabbages when still young and tender to prevent them from 'running to seed'.

winter crop that requires rich moist soil, seeds can be sown from mid-summer in cold areas, or late summer in warm regions. Although quite slow growing, swedes store well in a 'clamp', and the crop can be made to last for many months.

Turnips (*Brassica rapa*): Turnips are a winter crop and seeds should be sown in spring for early crop, or mid-summer for late crop.

Rich, moist soil produces good results, and a mulch of well-rotted manure topped by grass clippings will keep weeds down.

ROOT CROPS

Generally not as demanding on the soil as other crops, root crops need good drainage.

Beetroot (*Beta vulgaris*): Beetroot is best when picked and eaten young. It likes a rich soil, high in nitrogen, and poultry manure dug in prior to planting is beneficial. Add a sprinkling of lime also, mulch well once seedlings have reached 10cm

Root crops should not be grown in soil that has been enriched with fresh manures.

(4in) in height. Force growth along with regular feeding and watering, and begin pulling every second plant eight to ten weeks from sowing.

Carrots (*Daucus carota*): The average harvesting time for carrots is at least 16 weeks, and seeds can be sown from early spring in most areas. Successive outdoor sowing will maintain harvest.

Carrot seeds are very small, and the main problem is sowing them thinly enough — try mixing some seeds in a salt shaker with some dry sand.

Sprinkle this mix along a row and cover with light soil, then keep moist until germination. Even so, seedlings will need to be thinned to prevent overcrowding.

Well developed roots can be stored in a 'clamp' or sand box for winter use.

Parsnips (*Pastinaca sativa*): The distinctive taste of parsnips is either loved or hated. Follow the same planting procedure as for growing carrots. They need to be grown quickly and harvested when young, or they will develop a tough, stringy texture.

Lift when leaves die down and store in a 'clamp'. Lifting after a frost is thought to improve the flavour.

Potatoes (*Solanum tuberosum*): Generally because of space, potatoes are not grown in suburban vegetable gardens. However as they are so good, it is worthwhile devoting a section of the garden.

Nurseries sell seed potatoes in many varieties, or try planting leftover kitchen potatoes that have begun to sprout. Surprisingly, potatoes like quite rich, well-drained but moist soil, and can be grown all year round in temperate to hot zones. In cooler regions sowing can begin in spring after the frosts have finished.

When foliage appears mulch well, and continue mulching up to prevent potatoes emerging from beneath the ground — once exposed to light they turn green and cannot be eaten. Ensure they are lifted and stored before risk of frost.

Sweet potatoes (*Ipomoea batatas*): Sweet potatoes are very vitamin rich, but take a long time to grow and must have a long, hot summer. In cool regions it is hard to get good results because the growing season is too short.

Seed stock is hard to find, but tubers can be grown from bought produce that have been allowed to shoot. An average plant takes five months to mature.

VINE CROPS

Vine crops are best sown directly where the plants are to grow, and the most effective method is to create a small hill with a dish-shaped centre.

Place at least three seeds in this dish and keep lightly moist until germination. After a week, select the strongest plant, then

Vine crops such as melons require plenty of watering and regular feeding.

remove the remaining two.

Mulch well, taking care not to take the mulch too close to the stem, which can create too much humidity and cause a fungal disease.

Vine crops can be trained onto a trellis or wall (only those producing small crops like cucumbers) or allowed to ramble.

Cucumber (*Cucumis sativus*): Easy to grow in a wide range of soils and climates. In warm regions, cucumbers can be grown from seed sown directly in the ground, best reared under glass in cool regions.

Add some well-rotted manure and lime or dolomite before planting. Do not over-water during the germination period, but water well when plants are established. Shade from direct sunlight.

Pumpkins (*Cucurbita maxima*): To do well, pumpkins require a rich moist soil, protection from frost, and a long hot summer.

Sow seeds in early spring; in cool regions bring plants on under glass. Water and fed regularly throughout the growing season. Mulch around seedlings once established, as competing weeds will slow growth.

Although the smaller varieties may be ready for harvesting after four months, the larger types take longer.

Wait until the foliage and stems have withered before harvesting.

Squash, Marrow, Courgette/Zucchini (*Cucurbita pepo ovifera*): These fast-growing summer crops are grown easily from seed sown in early spring. Sheltered sunny sites give the best results.

Once established and mulched they require very little attention apart from regular watering. The flowers are also edible, but it is worth waiting for the squash.

Once the squash form, growth is rapid, so check daily, as regular harvesting encourages new growth.

Potatoes need plenty of ground space, they are useful for breaking up tough soils.

Zucchini is a heavy producer. Three or four plants are sufficient for the average family.

THE ONION FAMILY

This group is easy to grow and produces a good quantity in a small space.

No particular growing requirements are needed, and there are now varieties which will grow in all climates, even the warmest.

Chives (*Allium schoenoprasum*): Chives grow quickly in moderately rich, moist and well-drained soil. Grassy foliage produces pretty purple flower-heads which will self-seed for the following season.

Use sharp scissors to cut chives at ground level as needed.

Leeks (*Allium porrum*): Leeks need richer soil than other members of the allium family. They prefer a cool to cold climate, although they will grow in warmer areas if seeds are sown in autumn. Consider using plots vacated by early harvests of pea,

potato and salad crops.

Make a trench and sow seeds in the base, stems need blanching as the plants grow. This involves covering the stem base with soil to keep them white. Mulch well and water regularly.

Shallots (*Allium ascalonicum*): Shallots prefer cool growing conditions; warm regions should plant in autumn; cool regions plant in spring. The soil should be moderately rich, well drained, the seedlings thinned and mulched once established.

Harvest as foliage turns yellow, lift and lay in sun for 2-3 days, then store in cool dry place or pickle in vinegar.

PEAS AND BEANS

Both peas and beans have the same basic growing requirements. The soil for both needs to be rich with organic matter and well drained, with some lime or dolomite added prior to planting seeds.

French beans (*Phaseolus vulgaris*): Climbers are a good space saving crop for small gardens. These need moderately rich soil, lime should be added before planting.

Once seeds are established mulch and water well, then feed fortnightly once the flowers appear.

Harvest when beans are young and tender, as they will quickly become tough if left on the vine.

Successive sowing in warm climates will keep a good supply going.

Broad beans (*Vicia faba*): A cool climate crop which can be sown in spring for summer harvest, and allowed to mature as the weather cools in autumn.

Beans are heavy feeders and need plenty of ground space. Mulch seedlings well and water frequently during warm weather.

Once the pods begin to form, pinch back foliage tips to encourage faster maturing.

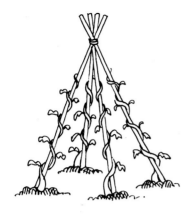 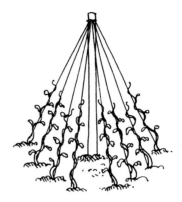

Two simple structures for supporting climbing beans :
(a) posts tied at the top; (b) string attached to a central pole.

Peas (*Pisum sativum*): Peas are a good cool season crop. Soil should be rich and sprinkled with dolomite before planting. Sow the main crop in spring, staking allows light and air to circulate around plants.

Keep well watered during dry spells. Depending on the variety, peas mature in 12 - 16 weeks. Crops are reduced if left on the vine, they are best if picked and eaten when young.

SUMMER CROPS

Salad crops including capsicum, eggplants, corn and tomatoes, are best grown in summer, even in warm regions. All require plenty of space, good rich soil and lots of summer sun to produce good results.

Capsicum (*Capsicum annum*): Plant early in spring since fruits need a long, hot summer to ripen fruits.

In cool regions wait for frosts to pass, then plant in a sheltered sunny site. Stake plants as the fruits form.

Mulch, water and feed plants well, pick late in the summer season.

Eggplant (*Solanum origerum*): Rich, well-drained soil is needed, and plants should be mulched and watered well in summer. Grow under glass in cool regions.

As the fruits begin to set, start a weekly feeding regime and maintain 4 - 6 fruits on each plant, this will encourage a larger and healthier crop. Harvesting can begin after 14 or 16 weeks.

Sweet corn (*Zea mays*): Corn needs plenty of space and good rich soil to be effective. Seeds should be sown directly into the ground, in a block of short rows for easy germination. In cool regions sow groups of 3 under glass in spring, then prick out the two weakest plants later.

When seedlings emerge mulch well, grass clippings help keep weeds down.

Water and feed regularly and start checking husks when the silks turn brown — do not leave ripe corn on the stalks or it will become woody.

Tomatoes (*Lycopersicon esculentum*): Tomatoes need as much sun and air as possible. In cold climates bring on seed-

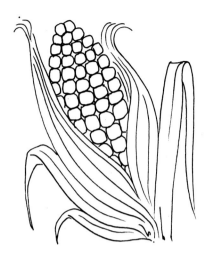

Sweet corn must be harvested when it is young and tender.

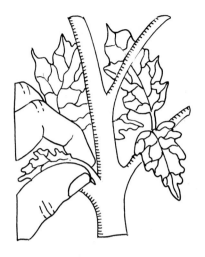

Pinch out the lateral growths of tomatoes to concentrate the yield.

lings under glass. Plant out in late spring in a warm, sheltered and sunny site for a summer crop.

Mulch around the young seedlings, and water regularly at ground level as plants can develop disease if foliage is constantly wet.

A larger crop is assured if the lateral growths are pinched back from an early stage, encouraging only fruiting stems. In warm climates well-grown tomatoes should be ready for picking after 12 weeks.

Perennials

Perennial crops should be grown in an area of their own, where they can be covered with a good mulch of well-rotted manure in winter while growth is dormant.

The most popular perennials are rhubarb, artichokes and asparagus, which emerge

Opposite: Allow tomatoes to ripen on the vine.

Corn is ready for harvesting when the silks turn brown.

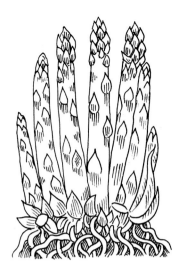

Asparagus is a worthwhile perennial crop in cooler climates.

from the ground in early spring then die back completely in winter.

Artichokes (*Cynara scolymus*): Freshly picked artichokes are so delicious that just a few plants in the garden are well worth the space.

They are best grown in temperate zones, resenting conditions that are either too hot or too cold. Fast growth is essential, so make sure the soil is well-drained, yet rich and moist.

Plant out on a sunny but sheltered site, water and feed regularly during the main growing seasons of spring and summer.

Asparagus (*Asparagus officinalis*): Asparagus require a hot summer and cold winter, although they can be grown quite successfully in most areas.

Make sure soil is rich before planting the crowns, and mulch well in winter. They are quite heavy feeders, so regular applications of liquid plant food will be beneficial.

Once spears emerge in spring regular harvesting will extend the season.

Rhubarb (*Rheum rhaponticum*): Rhubarb will produce vigorous stalks over many months if well tended.

Surface mulch in winter while crowns are dormant, using a well-rotted manure to enrich the ground.

In spring begin a regular water regime, as the stalks have a high water content. Continue mulching and watering through summer, and harvest the outside stems from late spring onwards.

Opposite: water rhubarb regularly, feed with a nitrogen-rich fetiliser to encourage rapid growth.

HARVESTING
& STORING

The best time to harvest vegetables is in the early morning or evening, when the sun is not directly shining on them. Always pick vegetables at their peak, and don't allow them to stay in the ground too long, becoming hard and woody.

Some root crops, such as carrots and parsnips, can be allowed to remain in the ground during cold weather, however the younger they are harvested, the more they will be tender and tasty.

Tomatoes can be picked just as they begin to turn red, then be allowed to ripen on a sunny windowsill. They can also be allowed to ripen on the vine, but take care the birds don't get to them first!

Alternate by picking every second lettuce in a row, to create a larger space between crops for the remaining lettuce to spread.

Every second carrot should also be pulled, making more room for the rest to grow.

Zucchini, which grow very rapidly, will turn into unpalatable marrows if not picked when young. In high summer it's best to check every day and see how they are progressing.

Sweet corn needs to be checked regularly, too, as it turns from being sweet and succulent to being woody virtually overnight.

Pick every second carrot in the row, leaving space for the remaining plants to continue growing.

The crop can be stored by freezing, pickling or bottling — to be enjoyed all year round.

Harvest crops in the late afternoon when the sun has left the garden.

As a rule, during harvesting, never leave picked vegetables standing in sun, where they will quickly soften and lose some of their nutritional value.

Pick crops for the kitchen as close to cooking or eating time as possible, to maximise nutrient value.

STORING THE YIELD

Certain vegetables can be stored success-fully for later use. Only store the best quality produce, not those with blemishes or soft spots.

Freezing: Trim, peel and blanch vegetables for a few minutes in boiling water. Place in an airtight freezer pack, or inside a plastic bag (extract as much air as possible).

Bottling: Good for fruit and vegetables, a brine (salt and water) or a syrup (sugar and water) solution is prepared and poured over the fruit or vegetables after they have been packed in clean glass jars.

The jars are then sealed to preserve the contents. Cooking times and temperatures are important to destroy bacteria, so always follow guides set out in a preserving recipe.

Drying: Fruit is peeled, sliced and dried on racks either in sun or a special drying oven.

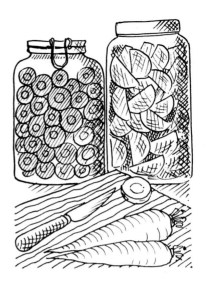

Bottling is an effective way of extending the crop.

Dry storage: Whole vegetables such as pumpkins, potatoes and onions are stored in a cool, dark and dry place. If possible potatoes should be packed so as not to touch each other.

Opposite: Pinch out lateral growth of tomatoes to increase the yield.

44

INDEX

VEGETABLE GARDENS